1

The
Domino
Heart

160201

The Domino Heart

by

Matthew Edison

Playwrights Canada Press
Toronto • Canada

Playwrights Canada Press

215 Spadina Ave., Suite 230, Toronto, Ontario CANADA M5T 2C7
416.703.0013   fax 416.408.3402
orders@playwrightscanada.com • www.playwrightscanada.com

Playwrights Canada Press acknowledges the support of the taxpayers of Canada and the province of Ontario through The Canada Council for the Arts and the Ontario Arts Council.

Cover photograph: Letizia Volpi
Cover design: JLArt
Production Editor: Mirka Zivanovic-Kosciuk

National Library of Canada Cataloguing in Publication

Edison, Matthew
    The domino heart / Matthew Edison.

A play.
ISBN 0-88754-728-1

    I. Title.

PS8509.D58D64 2004   C812'.6   C2004-902483-3

First edition: July 2004.
Printed and bound by Printco at Toronto, Canada.

For Jacqueline Edison.

Thank you to Rosemary, Raoul, David, Michael, Arwen, Kelly, Joanne, Rick, and Derek. And to Pam, Andy, Urjo, Mallory, Iris, Amy, Marjory, Katia, Hays, and John Sweeney. Thank you to Jack in the Black Theatre and Tarragon Theatre.

The Domino Heart was first produced by the Tarragon Theatre, Toronto in co-production with Jack in the Black Theatre, in March, 2003, with the following company:

CARA FORTREE	Rosemary Dunsmore
MORTIMER WRIGHT	David Fox
LEO JUAREZ	Raoul Bhaneja

Directed by Michael Kessler
Set Design by Kelly Wolf
Costume Design by Joanne Dente
Lighting Design by Rick Banville
Sound Design by Derek Bruce
Stage Managed by Arwen MacDonell

Characters & Setting

Part One: "The Living Room" CARA FORTREE, University Professor, early 40's. A cottage living room.

Part Two: "This Vital Fire" Reverend MORTIMER WRIGHT, Anglican Minister, nearing 70. A private hospital room, early morning, a few days prior to Part One.

Part Three: "The Horse's Mouth" LEO JUAREZ, Global Account Director of Lucas, Triggs & Berkoff Advertising, 33. A corporate office, Chicago, late evening, a few months later.

Part Four: "The Blind & Familiar" CARA FORTREE, a small hospital chapel, about a month since we last saw her.
The Voice of MORTIMER, or as he was left sitting, in a faint light.

Time

Present day.

Notes

LEO's opening lines of dialogue, translated from the German, read: "Yes…? Yes…?" "Good, thank you. I'd like to close that account now please and transfer it to… yes, all of it. Mm? That's right. As soon as possible please. Are you ready? Chase Manhattan Bank, Chicago. Corporate account number: 503…. Ready? 50310. Transit number 00476, 28093. Could you repeat it back to me please…? Mm-hm…. Excellent, thank you. What's your name?" "Sophia. You have a lovely voice, Sophia. Could you please have it transferred immediately? Thank you very much. Good-bye."

The transplant scar: A purple-red scar down the centre of the chest with two button-like scars below the central scar, and on either side (about two to three inches apart).

In answer to the inevitable question: "Who are they talking to?" I will only say, for my part, they are talking to themselves, they are talking to their best friend, to God, to the dead, and directly to the people in the room.

PART ONE

The Living Room

*A cottage living room. Flowers and cards lie about.
A square black case rests on the floor by a chair. Cards,
torn envelopes and a silver letter opener lie near by.*

*CARA is staring out a window. "Love is a Chain" by
Greg Brown plays on a record player. She wears
a black dress and a neck brace. A couple of bruises can
be seen. She holds a glass of red wine in one hand and
the bottle in the other. She drinks the last of the wine
in her glass and turns the stereo off before the song is
finished. She pours another glass. She rests the needle
to the beginning and listens again. She removes the
needle after a moment of listening and shuts off the
stereo.*

CARA   Yes. Well. No use thinking about it.

The irony of course is that it was Peter who wanted to
get the car with all the supposed safety features.
I was pushing for the, you know, I kept saying,
"I want the cute yellow one with the removable top."
(I remember thinking there was an opening for a little
joke, "Don't we all, dear," or something,) but Pete….
"We've gotta think of Gracie," he said. And it's true,
I wasn't. Well, not that our daughter would be – that
any of us would be killed in the car we were about to
buy. You just don't think of those kinds of things.

But he did. Peter did.

I remember once, here, at the cottage – Peter's parents
were visiting. At one point, Linda (Peter's mother)
went to bed and I went upstairs to check on our
daughter, Gracie. Peter and his father were left talking on the porch. I could hear them from the window
going on about the family of loons that had nested

themselves at the end of the lake. I sat in
a chair with Gracie for one of those late night
nursing's, burying my nose in her hair. George,
Peter's father, got to talking about Linda and it was
really quite sweet to hear how much he was still in
love with her. They'd been together, what… nearly
forty years? Anyway, at one point—and somewhat
out of the blue it seemed—he let go this deep sigh
and said, "I hope she dies before I do." And then
Peter, in a sort of tone of understanding, "I know."
And I couldn't, I mean, what was that? She wasn't
sick or anything. I thought, that's a terrible thing to
say! And then for Peter to agree as if, you know, as if
the same could be said for me. Well.

But, you see, I never understood love the way Peter
did. Now I, of course, *now*, but…

That is true love. I wouldn't wish life on anyone who
has lost… lost…, because you're as good as dead but
you're not dead. Yours is a death of a different kind.
A life of death. It is a life sentence. And you must live
it, each day, with a sort of hopeless Promethean
routine.

> *She removes her neck brace and carefully massages her
> neck.*

I don't know how he could have known that. Except
that he must have thought about it. If I had died or,
more likely…

Which brings me back to the car.

> *She rummages through her purse, finds some pills and
> chases a few back with an unhealthy gulp of wine.*

So! We bought the Volvo. And the irony, the not so
comical but nonetheless remarkably ironic thing was
that Gracie, thank God, wasn't in the car, I got out

with little more than a few scrapes and bruises and Peter was the one... who was killed.

"Several factors," they tell me: snow flurries, black ice, a pick-up truck with a load of steel pipes and... oh yes... a deer.

The deer stepped in front of the truck, the truck hit the deer, then we hit the back of the truck, which caused a steel pipe to come loose and go through the windshield... and Peter's head.

She looks at the stereo.

That song was on the radio.

This is what is known as the "chain of events," the police tell me, the chain of events that led to my husband being dead.

But maybe it started earlier, earlier in the evening. Or maybe it began some time ago.

We were arguing. We were in the midst of a heated but important argument which went off at that moment, in the car, but was planted long before we hit the truck that carried the pipes that killed Peter.

She finishes her wine. She pours another glass while continuing:

We were at a party. A big to-do at the museum. Peter's editor was having his sixtieth and his wife put together this Who's Who for a surprise party – Munro, MacLeod, Ondaatje – you know, a lot of them. Peter and I were mingling through the room, doing the usual, making more contact with the waiters than the guests, when Peter leaned into me and said, "Who's that?" And he pointed to a young man across the room who smiled and raised his glass when I looked over. "I don't know," I said. Which was a lie. Because that young man was a student of mine at the university and is the son of, I'm not saying whom, but a relatively well-known author. Let's call this young man… James.

Well. Okay. James and I had a very… brief affair that…

    Beat.

God. It was stupid.

    Beat.

A couple of years after Peter and I were married— before Gracie (Peter was on a book tour)—James would come into my office after class… ask me questions. He was a smart kid. Handsome in a romantic sort of way. I was flattered, I guess. One starts to miss the excitement that comes with something new and unknown. I started to look for myself in the eyes of this boy, for something to remind me of myself, when I was that age. And I found it because I wanted to.

It's not that I didn't think about it, about Peter, I did. I knew what I was doing but… I don't know… I wanted to betray myself: the honour student, the wife, the teacher. "She can be counted upon to be counted upon" my mother likes to say. I wanted to throw it all to the wind: who I was; everything I'd gained by being that person. I wanted to gamble it all. And I did. I ran from everything chasing me straight into the arms of… fancy.

I called it off with James the night before Peter returned. He took it better than I hoped, really. In fact, James didn't seem to mind all that much. Relieved, probably. Wouldn't have to risk losing his

GPA over a messy break-up scene on the quad. 92%.
He earned 78 of it on his own. It got him where he
wanted to go. Got him where I wanted him to go too:
away. But… there he was… our trouble.

I should never have told Peter. But, you see, at the
time, I was confused. I didn't know that I was still in
love with him. And I thought it would give me clarity
by telling him. We'll talk it out. Maybe we'll find out
his own part in my unhappiness. At the very least,
we'll have an open and honest relationship.

When Peter came home, he saw me in the living room
– he always looked at me like… his face just lit up,
you know? Like a sunflower. And then… it was as if
a cloud passed between us and everything faded
suddenly.

It made me shiver.

We sat down in the kitchen and I told him. I don't
know what I expected exactly. Anger. Yelling. An
argument of some kind. Instead, he was quiet for
a very long time. His tears – they just came down his
face. Everything was very still. His eyes were so
green. I'd forgotten.

I'll say that I love him.

And just as I was thinking that, I realised it was true.
Like something dropped into place and my heart, my
whole… being *awoke*. But the thought then of what
I might lose scared the shit out of me. It terrified me.

Oh God, I thought, I've made a mistake. I've made
a terrible mistake and I can't go back. Why did I tell
him? I should never have said a damn word! Please
let this work out. Please. If he gives us a second
chance… our lives could be… I'll make it up to him.
We'll be *happy*.

I put my hand on the table, "Peter, I'm sorry. It was stupid. I just… I'm really sorry. What can I do? What do you need?"

"You," he said.

You have me, Peter. For God sake, I'm right here.

And he stood up. "But I want you to understand how I feel," he said. And he held out his hand, "This is my heart." And he squeezed his fist around the blade of a knife and he pulled it through his hand.

She takes a sip of wine and puts the glass down.

Peter taught me about love.

She goes over to the black case next to the chair. She picks it up and sits, resting it on her lap.

We didn't talk about it much after that. Didn't have to really, we knew each other pretty well. It could live between us, in the quiet.

And we moved on in a way, I suppose. Actually we had some wonderful times. I became a mother and Peter was a born father. When Gracie had trouble sleeping, we'd put her in the car and we'd drive around the city for hours talking about this and that, our future. We got this cottage…. We had some wonderful times… and I guess I wanted to believe that things were better but really, really, they weren't. Not really. He was never quite the same person and he knew it. He was less open, more insecure. And I'd look at him and think, "I did that."

Yesterday I… I've been reading his journals. I found this one page…

She pulls a journal from a bag. Opens it to a marked page, reads…

"When you find someone, you give them a little bit of your heart and hope that they return with a little bit of theirs. Slowly, over time, or maybe all at once, you hold it entirely in your hands as an offering. The most vulnerable part of yourself. Because you trust that, more than anyone, they will be tender with it. But when they are not, when they are careless, they destroy the very part of you that was born in the moment you first let it go."

She closes the journal.

Never take love for granted. It's the most amateur mistake.

She puts the journal away.

So that night, at the party, with James, whom I hadn't seen since he left for Harvard, Peter figured it out. He knew.

"Who's that?" He said.

"Where?"

"There. With the glass."

Beat. She raises her glass.

Remember me, Cara?

Beat.

"I don't know who that is."

Beat.

You shouldn't have asked.

We were going to have a weekend together. That was the plan. "We need some time alone together. We'll go up to the cottage, after the party, leave Gracie with your mother."

"Peter, the roads," I said, "The cottage isn't even–

"Shh," he said. "Let's just do it."

And I was really looking forward to that.

But then the silence in the car was so loud! I couldn't – "What, Peter, what?!"

And he asked me. And I don't know why I resented it but I did.

"Why?! Why do you want to know?!"

"Because I do."

"What, exactly? If that was him? My fuck? Yes, okay Peter, yes! Okay?! That was him! *Can we move on with our lives now?* Can we?!"

And he was silent, and I thought, "Christ, what else can I do? Isn't it enough?! What else can I do?!" I told him he was being selfish. "You're keeping me prisoner with guilt," I said, "Grow up! THERE ARE WORSE THINGS FOR CHRIST SAKE!"

Beat. A little detached.

He said, "I'm sorry." And then we hit the ice and drove into the back of the truck and the pipe came through the windshield. And that was it. He was gone. In a heartbeat.

Pause.

The truth is, there aren't many things worse than being careless with someone's heart. That is unforgivable. It's just that we become used to it.

She puts down the case and clears the coffee table.

I've never really felt better by being forgiven, only glad that whomever I've hurt feels he still has room for me in his heart somewhere – which is maybe what I was after. But the guilt is still there, forgiveness doesn't change that.

In ten years he hadn't been able to work through it.

So, you see, maybe the argument was also a factor in the accident. Maybe, I don't know, his lack of concentration, his watery eyes. Maybe, in fact, the thing in me that led to my affair with that boy, so many years ago, was the first link in the "chain of events" that led to Peter's death.

Or maybe a deer just crossed the road at the wrong time.

She goes to the case, unclasps and opens it to reveal a brass urn. She removes the urn and places it in the centre of the coffee table. She looks at it.

You can't…. There's no use in trying to make sense of things. It's a lesson in futility.

That's what's sort of endearing about the church. It tries to make sense of things in spite of it all. There's structure. Rules to fall back on when you're lost. Direction, even.

Peter and I weren't very religious. We joined a sort of non denominational church when we moved here. United. We thought it would be good for Gracie and, actually, to be honest, we enjoyed going. You got to meet some of the people in the community and they'd say hi when they ran into you at the grocery store or the bank, it was nice.

We stopped going after a while, I don't know why. Gracie started school and Peter went to work on his new book. We were never really what you'd call devoted members of the congregation. Still, I'd miss it from time to time.

So it was a little odd sitting there today, listening to the service. People crying, telling amusing stories. The minister, trying to console us with "The peace of mind that *might* come with the *idea* of knowing that Peter is in a better place, whatever that is for *him*." If you go to a shrink with questions they'll answer you with questions; if you go to God with prayer he'll answer you with silence; if you go to a United Church you will get noncommittal ramblings. But at least they're trying.

And then Gracie, sitting beside me—she's seven—she looks at me and asks, "Are you, okay?" And I squeeze her hand and say, "Yes, are you?" And you know what she said, this little girl of mine? She said, "I don't think this is about Daddy. I think it's about us."

I believe that if God does exist, he will most likely be a child.

> *She moves back to the table, picking up the cards that she cleared off.*

She has Peter's heart.

Actually, that's not true. The paramedics found Peter's organ donor card with his licence. 43, no history of heart disease, he was a prime candidate. At first, I didn't want them to take it. It seemed…

unfair, insensitive. But then the idea that maybe he might live on, you know, somehow, in someone else... I don't know, that made me feel better. So I said: Okay. If I can see it. I'd like to see it.

So. That night, after the accident—I'm in another room in the hospital, this bereavement counsellor is talking to me and I'm on these tranquilizers—the door opens and this doctor comes in with a para- medic and a cooler. He asks me if I'm the wife. I say, yes, and he hands me a surgical mask and asks me to put it on. I do. He opens the cooler and there it is. Wrapped in gauze. Sitting on ice. Purple. Healthy. Alive.

I was only allowed to look at him for a moment. Belongs to someone else now.

The doctor said, "He's going to a good home." I said, "It's not how I thought it would look." And he said, "What, like a valentine?"

"No," I said, "just..."

And they left, rushing out the door. Gone.

> *Pause. She moves over to the urn and removes the top. She looks inside. Facetiously:*

Your heart's a Phoenix, Peter. Did you know that?

> *Colder.*

It's just a, you know... it's just a pump.

> *She holds out her hand.*

This is my heart.

She clenches her fist around the letter opener and calmly pulls the blade through her hand, with only a slight wince of pain. Blood runs from her hand. She holds it out over the opening of the urn, dripping onto his ashes.

I want you to know how I feel.

Blood drips steadily into the urn as lights fade.

PART TWO

This Vital Fire

*A private hospital room. Nearly four-thirty in the
morning. Moonlight pours in through a window.
There is an armchair and a small table downstage. On
the table is a near-completed letter and a pen.
Reverend Mortimer Wright (MORT) stands looking
out his window. He wears slippers, and a housecoat
over pyjamas.*

MORT   Wake up! We've been asleep for too long! Stretch and
feel how your soul has atrophied. Rub your eyes and
see again. This world is filled with miracles! And our
time is short!

A good start. I knew I had them. There's an art to
writing sermons and last Sunday's was, if I do say so
myself, a doozy. The trick is—I always say this to
young ministers—speak as if you're dying. Because
you are. "Wake up! Our time is short. It's now. It's
this moment. *This* one. Gone!" And I know they're listening because if you really listen you can *hear* people
listening. Fidgeting, I believe, arises from the natural
discomfort of truth sinking in. The occasional coughs,
the creaking of pews, these are good sounds – like
that buzzer that goes off in hockey when a goal is
scored. It means the puck's in the net.

"Look around this room," I say to them; and, of
course, no one does. "Wake up! Rub your eyes!
LOOK!" They don't know what to look at, "What
does he want?" I want you to see. "See what? What?"
And they look and they don't see and I know that
this world is in trouble.

He imitates a hockey player.

I get the pass. I deak the Deacon. I wind up. Each one of us is a prayer heard and answered… and wasted!

He indicates a slapshot and reports the play.

It rockets towards the net with such lightning truth that even Satan leaps from its path. Will he score one for Jesus? Wait for it… wait for it…

YES! HALLELU–

Suddenly, he is seized by a sharp pain in his chest. He takes a deep breath and sits. Sips some water. The pain subsides.

Hallelujah.

To God.

Not yet.

Another deep breath.

Live as if you're dying because you are.

In a few hours I'm going to have a new heart. The old one's given out. I like to think it's because I overused it.

It's a waiting game now while they "harvest the organ." They don't often call it a heart here in the transplant world, it's "the organ." Nancy, the organist at St. Paul's said, "Just make sure this one's in tune and try to keep the pipes clean." She likes to remonstrate with me for the years I consumed Bertie's smoked meat sandwiches without heeding a single of her warnings. "The heart has its own plans," I tell her, "it follows naught but itself." As if I were quoting someone else.

It's very controversial back home. Shouldn't a man of the cloth respect the fate God has handed him? After all, isn't this what I've been waiting for? Heaven and eternal paradise await me on the other side. I don't know about that. I have some questions to be perfectly honest about it but I like my job, I like raising people's spirits, as it were. I'm good at it and I get a lot of joy out of it. Nancy likes to tease me. She said, "Geez, Mortimer, what do ya wanna hang around here for? You've had nearly seventy good years with that heart of yours." I said, "I know, but I was given a lifetime guarantee." And she said, "No, Mort, no one is given that."

> *Beat.*

It's possible that my body, this church, may not accept the gift of this new *organ* so… if it's not to be, heaven and eternal paradise would be a nice runner-up.

We'll see. My prayer remains the same: for *harmony*.

> *He refers to a needlepoint sign.*

My mother made this sign for me when I was a kid. There's this little cowboy spinning a lasso and under him it reads: "Please be patient, God hasn't finished with me yet." It hung on my bedroom door for years. I found it in a box after my mother died and brought it to the church to hang on the door of my office. Whenever someone felt it necessary to discuss the issue of my having heart transplant surgery I just pointed to the sign.

I like to imagine that I am this little rancher; stuck at the age of five or so; trying to rope in the strays.

I used to manage this volunteer program to help babies who were orphaned. Some of these children suffered from addictions to alcohol and narcotics, carried down through the parents. (The word "withdrawal" wasn't even around the corner); their screams were terrible, they'd cry, their bodies were all purple and red; sometimes they'd break into seizure—they were a mess—and beyond holding them there wasn't much you could do, but already that was a lot. My job was to find volunteers to come into the basement of this church for a few hours each day and have them hold one of the babies. Just sit and hold them.

It wasn't easy getting volunteers and I don't blame them; it isn't a walk in the park. But then, love is not always a walk in the park. "If you hold them to your chest," I told my new soldiers of affection, "they can feel your warmth and hear your heartbeat – it's as important as *food*." Those that went the extra bit further and talked to them, stroked hair, kissed cheeks, dramatically improved the babies ability to cope with their afflictions.

People that are loved are healthier, happier, stronger people. Full stop.

What bothers me is, why do we think we need anything less when we're older? There are people in this world who are starved for love. I don't get it. There's a bottomless resource of the most valuable and powerful commodity in the world and still there are people going without. Do we deprive ourselves? Why don't we let it in? Okay, we don't like to burden people with our needs. But people want to love, they're waiting for the chance! Why deprive them of the opportunity to…. It is what we do best when we are at our best. And we do it naturally. Beautifully.

I'm sorry if I sound – I'm a preacher, it's an occupational hazard. When I was a young minister, they used to say to me, "Don't be a saint, Mortimer, you'll get crucified."

I remember a night at the centre: one of the babies
was crying and I took her outside onto the fire escape
to get some air. It was a clear night, like tonight, with
a full moon, and she just reached up to grab it. The
nurse here told me, she said, a lot of us do this when
we're young, before our minds have learned about
size and distance. We actually think we can pluck the
moon out of the sky and roll it around in our mouths.
I believe it's possible to stop and see people simply as
they are: wanting love and to be loved. Everything
boils down to this. But, like the moon, what we reach
for in the beginning out of instinct, we stop reaching
for in time, as we lose faith. And the faith required for
it is as simple as reaching up to grab it.

I'm scared about tomorrow, I'm not going to lie to
you. Not of dying – that's not – not of dying but of
not *living*. It should always be about the living.
There're too many people to meet, books to read,
places to go, things to learn. This is why I don't sleep.
I'm restless. Here it is now, what…

He looks at a clock.

Holy moly! Four-thirty.

Beat.

Soon.

Pause.

They'd kill me if they knew I was still up. Tried to
give me a sleeping pill. They said that patients about
to under-go – or *go under* is probably more accurate,
let's say *through* – patients about to go *through* major
surgery don't often sleep well. They are kept awake
by the impending and omnipresent question mark of
their own mortality. But I never sleep. Why sleep?
There's plenty of time for that later.

I told my lovely nurse, Janette, I said, "Janette, my body is God's temple and I'm afraid that I simply can't allow that pill to reside in my system. You understand." And God bless her lovely, naive, twenty-four year old heart, she did.

Only in a hospital would they want you to be well-rested so you can be wide awake for the anesthesiologist to put you back to sleep again.

She's very sweet, Janette. I've come to know her over the many visits here – I think she's sweet on me. Who can blame her? I came in tonight and she said "Well? The moment of truth, eh Reverend?" I said, "No, the moment of verisimilitude." She crinkled her nose, "You're gonna make me look that up, aren't ya?"

Her boyfriend, Wally, is studying to be an engineer out at Waterloo. She misses him of course and I like to ask what he's up to because I know she's dying to talk about him. Her eyes just light up. I see two small burning stars, and I think about that phrase, "windows to the soul."

He adds to the letter.

I don't know why I never found someone myself, got married. I thought I would; it just never seemed to happen when I was looking for it. Then, of course, when I wasn't…

Love really is like winning the lottery. You're ecstatic, all problems are suddenly made trivial, friends writhe in envy, and you can't believe that you got it. You pinch yourself and it's still there. "This can't be." So we test it. We push it to the limit. How real is this love? How true, how strong? Can it survive distance? Time? Betrayal? But why do we do this? Unless there's something in us that feels we don't deserve it.

Which reminds me of…

Pause.

Bailey Anne Foster.

He drinks some water.

Okay. Well, before I went into the ministry I was –
you may not believe this, as it's the kind of thing people usually say when there is absolutely no way of
proving it, but God as my witness, I had a flair with
the women. At least for a short time. It happened
rather suddenly in high school when I'd written a
poem for the school press. "Hidden Shadows", or
"Hid-in-Shadows", I think was the title – a sort of
Wallace Stevens, Edgar Poe flavour. Just the right
combination of scientific horror and overt sexuality to
unlock any sealed heart. So, anyway, I started getting
invited to these parties and meeting new people. And
all through this was the issue of my best friend,
Bailey Anne Foster.

Bailey and I were friends because our mothers were
friends. They had us at the same time and we only
lived a few doors apart. She was the quiet sort, which
suited me fine because I loved to talk – not that
I wasn't shy, I was actually quite shy with other people but with Bailey I could always talk. We were more
like brother and sister than anything else, but then….
Anyway, so: years later, and I write this poem and
suddenly I start getting invited to these, you know,
these parties. And I bring Bailey to the first couple
but, really, no one knew who she was and she never
seemed to be enjoying herself all that much.
So I didn't tell her about the next one. Or the next
one. And then she asked me one day, over lunch, she
says, "Are you going to Tracy Wainwright's party on
Friday?" I thought, oh geez, here we go.

Now, the main reason I didn't want Bailey to come was because Tracy Wainwright took dance classes with Maggie O'Loy and there was a good chance that Tracy would invite her. Maggie O'Loy—or "Oh boy" as she was referred to in smoking circles—she was this girl I'd had a crush on since the third grade. Black hair, pink cheeks, green eyes. How was I going to get anywhere with her if I arrive with Bailey? Besides, people were already teasing us about being a couple. What could I do? So I said, "Of course, Bailey. Actually Tracy just asked me to invite you."

So. We arrive at Tracy's party and there's Maggie standing in the kitchen just as beautiful as I'd remembered her but, you know… fuller. We weren't there three minutes when Maggie, out of the blue, comes up to me and says, "I read your poem, it's beautiful." (God as my witness.) Before I know it, there I am on the living room floor, dancing, sort of – clumsy, nervous, sweating – but I am completely in heaven. We talked and I made some jokes. I remember thinking to myself, "Hey, kid, you're doin' all right here." I had the whole room laughing at one point. Bailey wasn't feeling well and she wanted me to take her home. "In a minute," I kept saying. And she'd return after sixty seconds and say, "Okay, that's a minute, can we go now?" And I was getting frustrated. I mean, couldn't she just wait? "What am I your damn babysitter?!"

And then Tracy, who never missed an opportunity to exhibit her footing at the top rung of the social ladder, "Yeah, Bailey, I mean, I didn't even invite you."

Kids.

We didn't speak much after that.

Occasionally we'd bump into each other with a "Hello" or "How's your mother?" But not much.

Then, one day, about a year later, the phone rings. My mother comes into my room. She's crying and she says, "Bailey has died. She took her own life." Her note read, "I'm sorry but I'm so *tired*."

The thing I have to admit here is that I knew she had been abused, and I knew that she was in love with me. All of this I knew for many years. But we never talked about it so I pretended that I didn't. This doesn't mean that I was responsible for her death but it does mean that I was irresponsible with her life. And her love and friendship.

I couldn't move. For days I didn't get out of bed, didn't eat. I had made this movie in my head of me and Bailey, that ran all the way from the sandbox to that night at the party, and then to her lying in a bathtub of her own blood. I wound it back and played it in a loop, transfixed with a despair that began to overwhelm me.

He moves to the window, looks down.

Death is not about the dead. It's about the living.

Pause.

What I realised is that I was blind. That I had begun a pattern of blindfolding myself from a world that increasingly frightened me. I pretended not to notice, for instance, that Bailey had stopped laughing as much as she used to, was eating less; wearing long sleeves; turtle necks. It was as clear as day if you were looking but who was? Everyone would say later, "We didn't see it coming." But lying in my bed, numb with the loss of my friend, I faced the inevitable outcome as it played and replayed itself in my mind. And I just... I couldn't say to myself: you had no idea.

It was my aunt Brenda that stopped the projector, got me out of bed and got me going again. She signed me up as a volunteer to hold babies in the basement of our local church. I didn't want to do it but she forced me and thank God she did.

One of the many things I've learned holding these kids…

Hmm.

> *He adds to the letter. He pauses, continues writing for a long moment. Stops.*

We're born with this will to live. A fire, a vital fire—like a pilot light—so that even when hope is extinguished there is still… this spark within us to ignite the dying embers.

> *He folds the letter.*

I told the congregation last Sunday, I said, "We have to live, or die trying. And there is darkness," I tell them. "This world is flooded with darkness, but we don't have to go to sleep. When the blanket is thrown over our cage we should sing bloody murder!"

I ease off the gas, downshift, "Lest we forget, that in the "Paper, Rock, Scissors" game of life, Time beats everything, always." And I get a little bit of laughter, which is nice to have in church once in a while.

It's not easy to have compassion, real compassion, I know that, it's hard work. Especially for ourselves, I know. Heck, it's enough just to get out of bed some mornings without the weight of other people's lives to worry about. I can barely pick up the morning paper without some headline or photo of another dead child pressing down on me. True compassion isn't easy, and acts of compassion are even harder. So why should we bother?

Because we're doomed if we don't. We're doomed.

No more dead children, please. Please.

Beat.

There's this…

I've been following this war, you know, this one that's going on now, and in the paper last week there was a little column stuck somewhere between the obituaries and the stock pages. It started with a poem, this wonderful poem about gravity and stars and how things fall. It was a metaphor, you know, for what the poet, this girl, experienced… and what she…

Beat.

There are no words for what happened to her. And if there are, I don't want you to know them. I will only tell you that her story seems to me, still, the worst kind of hell I could possibly imagine for a person. She prayed for a miracle and only the devil in the uniform of a soldier appeared. At one point, it occurred to her that she could simply decide to stop breathing. It would be that easy, they had brought her so close to death. But something in her didn't want that. The moment she thought it, she says, she felt God, for the first time as she had never imagined because she never imagined that God lived in the form of love, inside herself, for herself. She pulled herself through the mud and escaped to Canada. And now she writes poetry about stars.

I think Bailey died because she couldn't find any love for herself. But no one helped her to find it. We weren't looking out for her. What will it cost us to open our eyes a little and take into our hearts and minds and arms the orphans of life's cruelty and smite their fears with the awesome power of unyielding love? What will it take?

Let me tell you: it takes nothing; a little courage.

> *He moves to the bedside table and retrieves two envelopes from the drawer.*

The heart is a muscle. Exercise it. Explore its limits.

> *He addresses one of the envelopes and inserts the letter.*

In these times of great weight we must, all of us, flex with every ounce of our being.

> *He folds the envelope with the letter in it and inserts it into the second envelope. He seals it and writes "Janette" on the outside. He rests it against the lamp on his bedside table and looks once more at the clock on the wall.*

Patience, Mortimer. God isn't finished with you yet.

> *He settles into his chair and stares out the window, mumbling.*

Don't go to sleep. Wake up… wake up…

> *Lights fade, except for the moonlight pouring through the window, which then too, slowly, fades.*

PART THREE

The Horse's Mouth

*Night. A minimalist-style office of the steel and cement
variety. LEO Juarez, a man of thirty-three, sits in
a chair behind his desk, swivelled away from us, facing
two monitors that show fluctuating international stock
markets. It appears as though he has lived in this room
for a couple of days (bottles of prescription drugs litter
his desk, an empty take-out food container or two, etc.)*

*At rise, LEO is conversing fluently in German into
a headset...*

LEO   Ja...? Ja...?

*He turns in his chair to write some numbers down on
a legal pad.*

*Gut. Danke. Ich mochte das kono auflosen und das
Guthaben auf... Alles. Ja. Ja, gleich. Sind Sie bereit? Chase
Manhattan Bank, Chicago. Korporative Konto Nummer
funf-null-drei – Bereit? Funf-nul-drei-eins-null.
Uberweising auf das Geschaftskonto: null-null-vier-sieben-
sechs, swei-achte-null-neune-drei. Konnten sie das bitte
wiederholen. MmHm.*

He checks his watch.

Ausgezeichnet. Vielen Dank. Wie heissen Sie?

He makes a note.

*Sophie. Sie haben eine schone Stimme, Sophie. Konnen sie
das bitte sefort machen. Vielen Dank. Auf viederhoren.*

*He hangs up. He grins, he moves to a humidor and
selects a small, expensive cigar. He continues in his
native tongue of Standard American English.*

Tree minutes and forty-two seconds.

He cuts his cigar.

Seventy-six thousand, eight hundred and forty-one dollars in three minutes and forty-two seconds.

Pours some cognac into a glass.

I've done better. More. In less.

He sniffs his cigar.

I challenge anyone to find two things that co-exist better than good cognac and a Davidoff cigar.

He pops a couple of pills and chases them with a swig of cognac.

What was I saying now? Oh yes, arbitraging (a little hobby of mine).

The simultaneous purchase and sale of the same or equivalent security in order to profit from price discrepancies in different markets.

He retrieves a revolver from his desk to use as a pointer, and stands between the two monitors.

Okay. Think of the World Economy as a giant heart and lung system. A very active yet completely unhealthy cardio respiratory nightmare. Okay? Now, think of money as oxygen (that shouldn't be hard). Look–

Refers to monitor.

This here, let's say, are the lungs, which intakes funds from raw materials—gold, oil, steel, whatever, —into the capillaries which would be, what, the various

international markets, okay? Where the money is
traded for–

Refers to other monitor.

Product.

Buying and Selling. Follow?

Refers to himself between the two monitors.

It's my job to make sure that a constant flow of
money and product is coursing through this ever
decaying body, the world we live in.

So. What arbitraging is, basically, is skimming oxygen
from the blood.

*He returns the revolver to his desk and pulls from
a drawer a new-button down shirt, still in it's packag-
ing. Over the next bit of speech, LEO unwraps the
new shirt and changes into it, throwing the one he was
wearing in the garbage. We see a surgical scar from
a heart transplant operation.*

This world floats on a rolling sea of dollars and cents.
A butterfly bats her wings in Malaysia and a hurri-
cane erupts off the coast of Mexico. You've gotta be
able to anticipate if you wanna make big money. The
storm—and I'll repeat this—he storm does not stop
for anyone.

This war right now is the proverbial butterfly. It's
affecting trade. People are feeling uncertain, anxious,
and the markets reflect this.

So: I look at Market A and I see it's low. I immediately
pick up the phone and place an order. While I'm on
hold with Market A, I pick up line two and simulta-
neously sell the shares to Market B, where the value

of the share is higher (at least for the moment). Before the market stabilizes, Market B buys it from me for a fraction more than I paid for it and a little less than they're going to sell it for. In other words, I buy a million dollars worth at a value of 10%, I sell it for 12 in an area that's still selling at 13 and I make a 2% profit. Follow? And all this time—and here's the punch line, folks—all this time, never actually using any of my own money.

Because as Market B is depositing the funds for the shares I've just sold them, Market A is entering the same account to retrieve the funds for the shares I've just bought. I've never actually owned the money, they're just trading through my account. One hand to another. And of course, Tim in accounting gets his cut for letting me play with the company's contingency fund. When the dust settles I'm left with a substantial piece of a very large pie. Seventy-six thousand, eight hundred and forty-one dollars in three minutes and forty-two seconds. For example.

Insider trading is one thing and I'm not saying I don't get tips. Of course I get tips, it comes with the job, it's a perk. But what I do is, I anticipate the markets' reaction by tapping into the collective unconscious. And it's like a tip being whispered into your ear by millions of people. Because I'm connected to the system. Veins and arteries lead from me, from this office, and branch into a complex network that reaches every part of this comatose world. And then it comes back. This is the heart. I'm in advertising.

If the exchange is not simultaneous thean your ass is bass and it's fishing season. The transaction happens very quickly and in this short period of time one either successfully navigates himself into a whole lot of money or into a whole lot of deep, deep shit. Prison for thirty years kinda shit. The risks are high and, like anything, that's the fun of it. Most of us have heart attacks by the time we're forty.

I was thirty-three.

He begins buttoning his shirt.

Wasn't Jesus about that age when he died? Can't remember – never paid much attention in church. Anyway, not important. I belong to a different church now. And I am a true believer. I have seen the light. God isn't dead, friends, he's alive and well and probably living in Saudi Arabia somewhere.

Those of you who don't believe me, who think, "Oh, he's just being cynical." Well…. Whatever makes you feel better.

He retrieves an electric razor and shaves.

I know, I'm sorry, I know, but don't shoot the messenger. Just trust me. The news I bring you is true, it's from the source. The horse's mouth.

Don't get me wrong, I count my lucky stars, every shiny one of them. I mean, I think we realise that in fact, yes, perhaps, practically, life is better with money than without, but—and you have to ask yourself this—what kind of life?

A word here to those of us at the top: if there is one thing we can learn from our history it's that the poor will, at some point, rise up and cut our heads off. Make no mistake, heads will roll. Rich and poor. It's just a matter of time. I know this because I've lived in both worlds. You have to, to understand anything about accountability – not that you have to understand anything about accountability – but it would be nice for a change.

He stops shaving and puts the razor away.

You've probably noticed I'm a bit of a mutt, a mixed breed. "He's almost white, I can't put my finger on it." Well, please, let me help you. My mother… she's Mexican and the Man who, what, fucked her, was a Ukrainian from the South side. A loan officer. He worked at a bank outside the projects where she was staying with her uncle. I'm not gonna get into all the details but the facts are these: her uncle would only let her stay with him if she worked and went to school. So she got a job cleaning office toilets and went to apply for a loan at the bank to, you know, for *tuition*. Well… my… my *daddy*, would only give it to her if she gave it back. "Do you understand me?" You know, with a little wink. So she got up and left the bank and on the way home, he pulled his car over and raped her.

Something like that. I only ever got pieces of that puzzle. And, of course, I am one of them.

Not that it was my fault or anything. But I should have been aborted.

I use to think she didn't, you know… like me. But I think we're just different people.

But, you know, I'm incredibly successful, now. So…

I am a divining rod for social need. If it doesn't gush forth from where I dig, I manufacture it. This is my area. I'm the Global Account Director for Lucas, Triggs & Berkoff. You may know of us, you've certainly been exposed to us. We're an advertising firm. A really, really big one.

Let me tell you something: growing up in poverty and fatherless, well… let's just say I was a little depressed most of the time. What I did was: I ate. I ate a lot. Junk food, anything. I got into drugs, I was huffin' glue, you name it. This is what you do when

your life is empty, when you're unhappy. You fill it
with something else. Even if it's only temporary, it
does bring a sort of… momentary contentment.

I remember looking at my mother one day in the
apartment – we were living on welfare – she slept on
the couch and watched TV for days on end. We were
watching, I don't know, re-runs of something retard-
ed and we just killed the last bag of potato chips.
Then this commercial comes on, bunch'a rich kids
throwin' a house party. It's set up like a beer ad,
right? (Lots of implied underage sex.) These guys are
in the backyard draining the pool. What do they fill it
with? Chips. A giant bowl of potato chips. Of course
there's two kids off in the corner who are just so in
love they have to share their own bag. I looked from
our empty bag on the floor, to the one on the TV, to
my mother lying on the couch. And what I realised
was that the world runs on the fuel people like my
mother and I provide. This fuel is need.

This was quite the epiphany for my thirteen-year-old
brain and it still holds true. When a company comes
to us with a product, we design a campaign telling
people why they need this product, and the company
pays me based on my reputation to tap into, or sum-
mon, the necessary desire required for the product to
have a "sustainable life."

Example. I work with all these guys, these suits,
right? What do they always talk about when they're
not going on about the grind, or who they banged in
Miami last week? They're talkin' about camping.
Hiking in the Adirondack's with their kids on the
weekend. How they're going to dust off the old tent
and spend a night under the stars roasting marshmallows, telling ghost stories. This image that they have,
this idea burrowing in their head, is like the junk food
I used to eat. It's potato chips. Something to fill the
hole. Those precious little childhood memories they

had when they went to summer camp and everything
was innocent and exciting. They want that back. And
they want the same for their kids. Of course. And
I smell it like franks on a stick.

So what I do is this: I sell 'em trucks. Take an ad, put
it in the prime-time news bracket, (CNN, maybe
a mid-day Golf match) and we sell them trucks—
jeeps, range rovers, SUVs—got it? Okay. We show
a dad behind the wheel with his kids in the back seat
of some SUV curbing around a dirt road in the moun-
tains. See? They don't roll over. I have his wife,
a cute, youngish, blond, smiling at him with pride.
Maybe she's even got a map open in front of her –
a little joke, right? Over this I lay in a voice, the best
friend, telling you how relaxing the weekend of
roughing it is going to be inside this luxurious,
patent-leather monster of a machine that climbs over
boulders and fallen trees at the shift of a gear. The
world at your fingertips, the voice might say, as the
back of the truck opens up to reveal a Coleman stove,
marshmallows, fishing poles, a tackle box – and, oh,
by the way? "You deserve it." As the possibility of
seeing yourself in this truck begins to dawn, I'll drop
in a standard list of operating features, read with
a let's get down and fuck quality that makes you forget we're talking about operating features (think
Barry White). The ad will close with the family sitting
around the campfire laughing, maybe a kid tucked
into his sleeping bag. The camera pulls back as if to
say, and what brought them together? What brought
them to this paradise? And then the truck, looking on
protectively, *fatherly* even, "I did." Who knows,
maybe a shooting star passes in the reflection of
a window, lands on the truck's steel name plate:
BRAVADO. "Because you had the courage to go after
a dream."

And, while the show they were watching tunes back
in, they can't seem to shake this image, this picture of

themselves standing at the edge of the lake with their son, their daughter, their wife, looking at them in that special way, as if to say…. You are my whole world.

And that's where I have them. I own them. They think the opposite. The truth is: I own them.

That's the Trojan Horse aspect of the advertising medium. It's a gem. What's really great is that everyone seems to know they're being manipulated but, as it turns out, no one cares. People think they're immune, and of course we let them think that.

Some of the corporate branding has become totally shameless, if you ask me. They don't even camouflage it anymore. Soap called "Innocence," Luggage called "Escape." There's no imagination.

He stops, thinks.

Hmm.

He writes down on a sticky note…

"Imagination."

Can you see the hook? You'll feel it when you bite.

He sticks the note to his computer screen. Pause.

The guy who used to have this job, Adam Holtzstein—he was forty-seven, I was twenty-six—he thought he did everything right, right? He gave to charities, did volunteer work, he never fooled around on his wife – you know the guy. Hell, he brought me into this place, if it weren't for him, I'd still be working on the floor. So, I get the call from Triggs that he's out and I'm in. And on that day, I'm in the washroom, I hear him crying. He's cleared out his desk and I see his box at the bottom of the stall. I say,

"Adam, you okay?" You know, he did a lot for me, I don't want the guy to go jumpin' through a window or anything. Anyway, he shouts back from the stall, "Go fuck yourself, Juarez!" (That's me.) "Come on, Adam, pull yourself together. Be a man, for Christ sake!"

And he didn't like that so much. He charged outta the stall, grabbed me by the throat, started yellin' all kinds'a shit, "Your mother's a Spic whore" and blah, blah, blah. And he's sweating and his face and eyes are all red and people are coming in and calling for security – that's when it occurs to me: he actually expected there to be some kind of equilibrium in the world where people, good and bad, got what they deserved. And he felt he deserved some good. Of course. But what could I tell him?

This is a fisherman caught on his own line.

Adam's squirming on the bathroom floor, struggling to get up and fight, it's embarrassing. His own friends holding him down – the look on their faces like, where the hell did this come from? He was always so nice. But I mean, really, I had to ask, "Why do you think you deserve better, Adam? 'Cause you've been a good boy? *That does not mean a shoe shiner's fart in the world of things*! How could you work a day in your life in this business and honestly believe that shit?! Seriously, do yourself a favour and stop acting like you alone have drawn the short fuckin' straw or something! Grow up! Be a man! This is the world you live in!"

Pause.

Then I washed my hands and left. And, honestly, I think that was the best thing anyone could've told him.

He coughs.

The mystery of where we are headed is only a mystery to those who still believe there is someone at the wheel. The rest have either submitted to the voyage or jumped ship. Or, as in Adam's case (and undoubtedly my own) slipped. And now just bob mercilessly in life's, what... salty wake.

Hey. I don't pretend to have it all figured out. I just do. It's why I'm successful at my job. I paint a picture of the world people think they want; then they walk into it and accept it as their own. But it's all illusion. It's slight of hand. It's a lie.

He coughs again.

The two things people notice most when they don't have them? Love and Money. But you see, the thing is, Money is tangible, okay? You can get it. If you have a knife, you can get Money. If you're clever you can acquire it, okay? But nothing you have – even Money – do you understand what I'm saying? All the tea in China will not guarantee you the other.

Look: you can't escape it. You have to buy this shit. And, really, you've got other things to worry about. So... so, why do I care?

I don't like this world. I have a very clear view of it's workings and from up here it resembles something not unlike a dead–

He coughs.

A dead–

Another cough.

*He grabs his arm and falls to his knees. After
a moment, he takes a slow, deep breath in. He drinks
some water, takes a couple of pills, recovers.*

I don't…

My mother. I don't understand her. I suppose that's
not uncommon.

Pause.

The thing is, I've spent my life… trying to, to, every
cent, I don't even own a – everything, all the money –
do you understand? For her.

I'm in the hospital, about to go into surgery… she
walks in – she's wearing the same *goddamn* sweater
she's worn for twenty years. Because, after all, what
would it—all of this—have been for, if not…? I mean,
I've worked hard. I've worked very, very hard to suc-
ceed in this… game. So just… you know, a coat!
Something!

"Thank you. You've been a good son, Leo…. You're a
good person."

But I'm not really.

Pause.

I should tell you that I hoped I would be wrong, that
strings would not be pulled simply because I could
afford to have them pulled. But I wasn't wrong. And
now, here I am with new life and—I feel I should tell
you—smoking, drinking, uppers, downers, salty
food, MSG, you name it. I'm supposed to be taking
these immunosuppressive drugs, but, well… sometimes I… wait.

I know, I know, I'm what? Undeserving? You're right.
But I think it proves a point, don't you?

After the attack this nurse wheels me into a private
room, it's got flowers, chocolates, DVD player – the
works. *Two minutes*, this Doctor shows up (Ever had
that happen?) Carl. Not "Doctor this" or "Doctor
that" just, "Carl." Like we're already friends, right?
He explains to me, he says, my heart is severely dam-
aged and would need to be replaced. He starts in on
how in order to get a heart the person has to be clini-
cally brain dead. I'm laughing, "Carl. Throw a stone
for Christ sake." Then he starts whining about the
position of the hospital, "There's supposed to be a
waiting list, a year to two years he tells me, and he's
fond of saying that no one, absolutely no one, is given
special treatment in this respect.

He grins.

Well.

You see, I'm a valued resource at the firm. To lose me
is to lose money. I'm attached to a number of big
accounts. If I go, they go. So: I'm in my room watching a flick, I get a call from Warren Ainsley, the firm's
legal associate. I'm not to worry, he says, "There's a
clinic near the Canadian border, they're taking care of
it." I said, "But what about the waiting lists?" "Don't
worry, Leo, you'll be back on your feet in a couple of
months."

Three Days Later I'm on a table in prep for
a "Domino Transplant Operation." This is an organ—
okay, and get this—that has already been transplant-
ed once before. Some guy gets killed they give it to
some other poor bastard who dies on the table or
whatever and then it domino's down the line to who-
ever's next. And would you believe? Lo and behold:

the buck stopped here. Is this the world we live in, I ask myself? Well, it turns out, yes. Yes it is.

Desperation, Survival, Economy. One heart, three bodies. Ba-boom, ba-boom, ba-boom.

I wonder what the guy would have thought of his heart bouncing around from body to body like a ten-dollar hooker?

You can't escape it. When you take a shower, get ready for bed, when you put your shirt on in the morning, there it is, pounding away under your ribs. And it was just beating in somebody else. What kind of world is this? The Lord taketh and the Lord giveth back again? Where's the sense in anything? I mean, where's the Goddamn sense that someone like me should get this heart?! Can somebody please explain this to me?! Can somebody explain why my mother is raped at 17 and gives birth to *this*?! This...

    Pause.

Anyone?

    Pause.

She'll never say it of course. But I know.

    Pause.

I know.

    Pause. Daylight is creeping in.

After the operation, I'm lying in the bed, the hospital bed, and I hear this beep-beep... beep-beep... beep-beep. I've been asleep for... wake up.... My eyes flutter open and the room is bright. What is this? Where am I? Beep-beep... beep-beep.... A hospital. Was I in

an accident? A car accident. But I don't own a car.
Wake up. Then I feel my mother holding my hand,
squeezing it, I know it's her (the dry skin, the callus-
es). And these thoughts are running through my
head: I'm sorry, forgive me – but for what? Why?
I wanna... I want to say that I love her.

She leans over and kisses me on the forehead. Her
tears fall on my face, roll down my neck into the pil-
low. I squeeze her hand. She looks at me.

And then I see it: my face in her eyes staring back at
me. And, there, just behind that reflected face is this
little hole of resentment... and I know that I can
never fill it. I will never fill it.

"How are you feeling?" She asks me.

"Like a million bucks," I tell her. "Like a million, million bucks."

He holds out his bottle of pills.

My life in my hand.

*He puts it away and retrieves a fresh tie. He begins
tying it.*

Things are easier thought than said, and they're easier
said than done. But I'm in the business of thought
power. And I want you to know that the people you
buy from do not care about you or the health or edu-
cation of your kids, or the environment, or inner-city
violence, or the third world, because they are not
designed to care. They are designed to make Money.
This is nothing new. But to make Money we need
your trust and we are lying to you to get it. A lot of
people with power do not want a better world they
want a tin can with legs and arms that can be filled
and emptied and filled and emptied until the soul is

rusted out. If it makes you feel better to tell yourself that I'm just being cynical, than you tell yourself that. If it makes you feel better. But I know this world. I've got my finger on the pulse and it's racing.

He wets the end of another cigar with his mouth.

Don't be fooled. Trust me, it's the truth. From the horse's mouth.

He takes the revolver from his desk and raises it, pointing it toward his mouth. He pulls the trigger. A flame sparks alive from the muzzle of the barrel, from which, LEO lights his cigar. He grins, returns the revolver/ lighter to the desk and turns the cigar in his mouth. Once more, he sets the ball bearings in motion and sits in his chair. Lights begin to fade slowly as he turns around; whistling, "If I only had a heart."

PART FOUR

The Blind & Familiar

*Hospital sounds: machines, intercom pages, et cetera,
fade to a room tone. Lights rise on CARA, sitting in
the pew of a small hospital chapel. She wears a coat
and holds her purse in her lap. A suitcase sits near by.
On the side wall there is a modern stained-glass window of the Sacred Heart.*

CARA   Today is the first day of spring. It is also the first day
of the rest of my life, I'm told. They're sending me
home today, from the hospital.

I love the smell of spring. The air seems crisper.
Sweeter. The flowers blooming, I suppose. But more
than that there's the smell of newness, don't you
think? Of possibilities?

I used to get very creative around this time of year.
I needed to stretch after a long sleep. I'd have this
rekindled urge to paint or write poetry. I'd drive to
Loomis & Toles and buy large frames of canvas, tubes
of cadmium red and cobalt blue. Slopping it on, I did-
n't care, whatever felt right. I loved it when I was
younger I don't know why I.... Trees. I used to
paint a lot of trees. I identified with them in a way, I
suppose.

I read this story in the paper a while back and – you
know the lights they put up in the trees that line the
main avenues? Well, an ecologist wrote a letter to the
city asking them to "please remove the lights because
the trees have not had a decent night's sleep since
Christmas."

Life's funny. Funny peculiar.

Pause.

I took some pills. I took a lot of pills. And I chased them with a half-bottle of vodka.

Three days ago.

I shouldn't have loved him so much. I'd hurt less. It humiliates me to be that woman. That woman who's so dependant that her life means so little without her man. "What is this?" I keep asking myself. "How did I get so lost? I was someone before he came along, who was I?" I'm still her but… I've been changed. He changed me. I'm someone else now, you know? And I can't go back. You can't ever go back.

I couldn't stop crying. My eyes were swollen, my face was raw from the salt and the rubbing. "Find strength!" Be stronger than this, Cara! Think of Gracie, think of your daughter, for Pete's sake… for Peter's sake. For your sake."

But how? I'm empty. Something from nothing? How do you do it? Of course, there's a lot to be thankful for but you don't see that. You think of all the things: your family, your friends… your daughter who needs you but… you're overwhelmed by a tide of numbness and it washes over everything. You look back and everything's gone, carried away; floating debris. You see the ruins where your life was built and you remember that just a moment ago it stood there, monumental, as if nothing could touch it. Gone.

I undertook to track down the man who had received Peter's heart. I wanted to know if I could… see him, Peter, in the eyes of this other person. Maybe his heart somehow lived more than just physically – I know, silly, well that's what I wanted to find out. Maybe I was looking for closure, I don't know. Anyhow, he died.

Something during the operation.

It's not easy to find the right heart. There has to be a perfect match. It has to be compatible or the body rejects it. Peter's heart was cleared for a Domino Transplant procedure. "Domino." What a world.

I don't know why I can't move on like other people. Inadequate coping skills, I'm told. I tried to find this other person, this "third man," but I couldn't. And I began to feel very lonely, listening to a therapist explain why it was uncharitable of me to be disappointed about not finding this guy whose life is sustained by my dead husband. After all, what about them? What about what they want?

But they've got what they want. They got another chance. What about me? I just wanted to tell them about Peter. We're connected by him. How come we can't meet each other and hold each other for a...?

The university gave me a leave of absence, my mother moved in "to help." I was a wreck. "Get yourself together," she said. "This is childish! Gracie doesn't have a father anymore; she needs a mother." I persuaded her to go home, to take Gracie. I didn't want her to see me like this. I promised I'd see someone, get help. I did see a bereavement specialist, I took medication – I just, I couldn't do it anymore. I was so... very tired. You know?

So I returned home, put on a Ravel concerto, dashed off a note for my lawyer, and a letter for Gracie, and I... embraced the pills. I know, it was selfish and... but really I just couldn't think of anything but sleep.

I remember a moment of consciousness in the ambulance. Then, apparently, I fell into a coma for 31 hours. So I guess I did get some sleep.

I remember when I was pregnant with Gracie and the nights I prayed my baby would be healthy, without complications. But life is complicated. Sometimes it feels as if, with all this new technology and with everyone trying to uncover the secrets, that there's nothing left to wonder at. But life, death, you know, it's comforting not to know everything.

She moves to the window.

Did you know that there are some colours of stained glass, for example, that can't be duplicated? You'd think with all the advances in science we could reproduce something as simple as a certain colour of glass, but we can't. There are cathedrals and churches all over the world that have broken, drafty windows because they can't be replaced. I like to hear things like that. It's humbling.

Isn't this a cute chapel? Two young people were married here yesterday. She was badly burned—a kitchen fire, I think—she had to wear some kind of protective something-or-other. Apparently she was quite beautiful, but then they always say that about people who have been burned, don't they? I mean, I'm sure she didn't look worse. I just find it ironic that those people who claim that beauty is not important are usually the first to say, "And remember how beautiful she was?" As if it would, somehow, be less tragic if she had been ugly.

Beauty is important.

There is a booklet here in the hospital about corrective eye surgery. It says that patients who have been blind since birth and have had the surgery, often fall into depressions following the operation. For the first time, they understand what the seeing world considers beautiful and it scares them. They see themselves reflected in a mirror and they fear they are not what other people want or like. So, apparently, they walk around with their eyes shut, reverting to the world of the blind and familiar.

I like that phrase. "Reverting to the world of the blind and familiar." I think that's what I was doing before the pills. Now… now I must force myself to look. I've awakened with a new life, new eyes, and I have to learn to see again, to live again.

She digs into her purse.

I was thinking about this, about my daughter and this life in front of us if I could find the strength to accept it. But, to be honest, I didn't think I could.

She pulls an envelope from her purse.

They say about people who've survived suicide that there is a moment after you've, whatever, stepped off the ledge, a moment where it's too late and you can't go back, and in that moment, they say, most survivors claim to have changed their minds. Well… I can't say that I actually had that moment but I have it now. I count my lucky stars. My daughter, Gracie. And Reverend Mortimer Wright.

He left me this letter on his bedside table in his hospital room. It was addressed to the donor's family should he die during the operation. It was here, the day I emerged from my coma, more than three months after he wrote it. My mother said it must have gotten lost in the mail but there was no stamp, so someone must have delivered it. But who? No one here seems to know anything about it. Now, that's a little spooky. I'm not usually one to leap to mythical explanations for things but, you have to admit, that's a little spooky.

I open the envelope. Just a letter. I don't know how else to say this – it was as if God were speaking to me. I know he was in the business, but I don't mean it like that. It was like... someone saying the very things I needed to hear in order to have the strength to lift myself out of bed. It was like he was in the room with me, and I... I just... wept.

She reads aloud.

Hello. My name is Mortimer Wright. I want you to know, first of all, that I love you...

The following speech is spoken by MORTIMER.

If there's a window in the room where you are reading this, and you feel up to it, I recommend pulling the curtains aside and letting the air in. Even plants need a bit of light and you can't read in the dark.

Beat.

And now I have to believe in miracles.

Pause.

I miss Peter. I miss him.

Sometimes I'd be in the corner store and I'd feel his breath on the back of my neck. I'd turn around... nothing. The clerk, just looking at me, my tears. I must have seemed crazy. I would think, am I? It's frightening to feel how much someone has grown inside you; how much of yourself is held together with the glue of other people.

I feel better. But there's a lot of reconstructive work to do. It's only natural after a part of you has fallen away. A very lovely part. That I'll miss.

Peter was answering some question from an interviewer on the radio once. And I guess the interviewer had imagined these were challenging questions on the subjects of life and death, and Peter, you know, he was a very clever man. At one point, the interviewer said, as if jokingly, "Alright then, Mr. Fortree, what, philosophically, do you think is the answer to everything." You know, with a little, "Eh, smart ass?"

Without hesitating, Peter answered, simply: "Balance."

Balance. Of course.

I feel like the first sprout breaking through cold earth and searching for the sun, for warmth, for home.

She begins to get her things together.

There are trees in Peru called Walking Palms. They look like arms with the fingers of the hand sunk slightly into the earth. These fingers are the roots, and I like to imagine as the sun moves across the sky, the roots pick up, one by one, like long, thin, Dali-esque legs and walk the tree towards the light.

I think Gracie and I might take a trip to Peru, if she'd like. Paint the trees. Talk. Laugh. Count some stars.

After all, our life is this moment. This one. Gone. In a heartbeat.

She smiles and goes.

Curtain.

Matthew Edison is an actor and writer living in Toronto. *The Domino Heart* is his first play. He is a graduate of Canterbury Arts High School in Ottawa and the Stella Adler Conservatory of Acting in New York City.

The Domino Heart is Matthew Edison's first play. As an actor, he has worked with Tarragon Theatre (*Midnight Sun*), Soulpepper Theatre, CanStage and the Shaw Festival. Recent credits include *The Winter's Tale* at the National Arts Centre and *Proof* at CanStage. *The Domino Heart* was developed by Jack in the Black Theatre led by artistic director Michael Kessler, who directed the co-production. In the fall of 2001 Matthew Edison directed Jacob Richmond's *The Qualities of Zero* in Tarragon's Extra Space. He received a Dora nomination for direction and the show also received a Dora nomination for outstanding production.